THE GIFTED ROSE

THE
GIFTED ROSE

*The Pleasure of Creating and the Joy of
Giving Rose-Scented Gifts*

JUDITH MAAS RHEINGOLD

ILLUSTRATIONS BY
CATHERINE ROSE CROWTHER

HEARST BOOKS
NEW YORK

This book could not have been written
without the help of Howard Rheingold, Esther Mitgang, Rita Aero,
and Catherine Rose Crowther. I would like to give my special thanks to
Patricia Stapley, Patti Graham, Betty Rappaport, Susan Friedman,
Elizabeth McCaughey, Aaron Stapley, Marie Maas, and
Geraldine Rheingold for their counsel and support.

It is the policy of William Morrow and Company, Inc.,
and its imprints and affiliates, recognizing the importance of
preserving what has been written, to print the books we publish
on acid-free paper, and we exert our best efforts to that end.

Library of Congress Cataloging-in-Publication Data

Rheingold, Judith Maas.
The gifted rose : the pleasure of creating and the joy of giving rose-scented gifts / Judith
Mass Rheingold : illustrations by Catherine Rose Crowther.
p.   cm.
ISBN 0-688-11146-7
1. Potpourris (Scented floral mixtures) 2. Roses. 3. Flowers–oDrying I. Title.
TT899.4.R44   1992
745.92–dc20
91-45879
CIP
Printed in Singapore

First Edition

1 3 5 7 9 10 8 6 4 2

F Y
PRODUCTIONS

DEDICATED TO

MY BEST HELPER ∼ MY LITTLE ROSEBUD

MAMIE RHEINGOLD

CONTENTS

THE FINE ART OF ROSE CRAFT

❧ I am an enthusiastic rosarian. I adore anything and everything having to do with these marvelously versatile blooming plants — growing them, smelling them, gazing lovingly at them, decorating my home with their blossoms, and using them to make heaven-scented potpourris, sweetly styled sachets, and, of course, drenching myself in their glorious fragrance.

When I moved with my husband and our young daughter from a flat in San Francisco to our new home in Marin County, we received three rosebushes as housewarming gifts. At the time, neither my husband nor I had experience growing roses — we were so rose-naive that we even cut off the metal nursery tags that identified each plant! We planted the rosebushes rather haphazardly, yet, lo' and behold, we reaped rosy rewards the following spring and have been rose-struck ever since.

I was so overwhelmed and proud of the abundant harvest of roses from our first bushes that I didn't want to part with even a single bloom. I gathered the precious petals as they dropped off the blossoms and made potpourri and sachets. I dried baby rosebuds in my microwave and used them to decorate my hats and shoes. Eventually, I ran out of nooks to stash my containers of potpourri, corners to hang-dry bouquets, and safe countertops to flat-dry single flowers. So, I began to dream up other ideas for using my garden's rosy remains, and our roses became three times blessed; first, appreciated growing to full bloom in the garden, then, cut and displayed lavishly as floral arrangements, and finally, reincarnated as rose-scented gifts.

As I experimented I jotted down recipes and gift ideas. I learned to dry delicate buds and blooms quickly in my microwave oven, to make long-lasting "wet" potpourri, and to design rose-scented jewelry to wear. Whenever I needed a gift for a birthday, anniversary, or special occasion, I would browse through my notes seeking inspiration for the perfect present, and I always found it. The recipes and formulas in this book are my tried-and-true favorites. Each of the nine projects will show you how to enjoyably transform yourself into a master at rose craftsmanship.

The one-of-a-kind projects in *The Gifted Rose* will introduce you to roses in their three commonly available forms — fresh, dried, and extracted as an essential oil. All of the gifts use living roses, even if they are not the main ingredient, they are a dashing garni or a charming decoration. I realize that many of you do not live in a climate that allows you to have year-round roses, or in a home with space to grow your own rosebushes. Fortunately, these are not necessary to enjoy

Miniatures

Tea Rose   Long Stem   Garden Rose

creating and giving rosy keepsakes. I have narrowed the very large field of common roses down to four types you can always find fresh at your local florist — miniature, tea, long stem, and garden. When you begin to assemble the ingredients for your rose gifts, refer to the painting of these four rose types that appears here.

Several of the ideas in this book use commercially dried roses either as buds or as potpourri. These prepackaged roses can be found in gift boutiques and stationery stores. Other recipes call for essential oil of rose, by far the most popular of all the essential floral oils available. Essential oil of rose is readily available in health food stores, pharmacies, and beauty supply stores, but should you have difficulty finding oil of rose or any of the other ingredients in this book, I have provided a mail-order source guide to reliable suppliers.

Once you have taken the care and love to make these wonderful gifts, they deserve to be wrapped with flair and imagination. After all, a gorgeously wrapped present makes a difference! You will enjoy putting together the special gift presentations I have fashioned for each project — interestingly woven straw baskets, personalized gift boxes, and the pretty gift bags of paper and cloth topped with French wire ribbon bows are sure to be kept and used again and again. Your friends will be delighted by the results, as mine always are.

I hope *The Gifted Rose* will be an inspiration to rose lovers everywhere, and in the time-honored tradition of giving flowers as a token of love and appreciation, I present this gift of roses to all of you.

SLEEPING BEAUTY'S
SCENTED LINENS

‿ Sleeping Beauty's Scented Linens are the next best thing to sleeping on a bed of rose petals. The favored recipient of this special gift has only to touch a few drops of rose oil to a linen towel or napkin and toss it into the dryer with freshly laundered sheets and towels. The linens will be permeated with a heavenly rose scent — a fleeting floral keepsake to be cherished when opening a linen closet or climbing into bed at night.

Small cream-colored note card, 4 inches x 2 1/2 inches
Rubber-stamp alphabet (peg alphabet set, no. 5)
Red ink stamp pad
6 fresh red tea roses
4 fresh long-stemmed orange-blend roses
1/2-ounce bottle rose oil with dropper
18 inches pink-and-green variegated French wire ribbon,
  3/4 inch wide
White gift box, 6 inches long x 4 inches wide x 2 inches
  deep

1 sheet rose-pink tissue paper
Fine-linen finger towel or table napkin
1 yard pink-and-green variegated French wire ribbon,
* 1 1/2 inches wide*
Sprig of fresh rosemary

 ∾ On the cream-colored note card, hand-stamp these simple instructions: "Touch ten drops of rose oil to this table napkin and put it in the dryer with your bed linens or bath towels to scent them with roses."

 ∾ I think the hand-stamped look is charming, so I don't worry too much about trying to align the letters in each word. I do, however, plan the layout of the words on the card to avoid an uneven or cramped appearance. Practice on a piece of scrap paper first. When you feel comfortable with the technique and your design, proceed to make the card.

 ∾ Prepare the tea roses for drying by cutting off the stems almost to the bud, leaving just a tiny bit, about one-quarter inch. Trim the long-stemmed roses to the length of the gift box, about six inches from bloom to stem end.

 ∾ Dry the two types of roses separately. Because of the size difference of the blossoms, the tea roses will dry more quickly than their long-stemmed sisters.

 ∾ Lay the tea roses on a paper towel and place in the micro-wave set to high. The drying process will take about three minutes,

depending on the power of your microwave oven. Fresh roses give off moisture as they dry, creating a cloud of steam that slows the drying process, so stop the oven and open the door every thirty seconds to allow any steam that has accumulated to escape. After the first two minutes, check to be sure the blooms aren't over-drying and becoming brittle. When the blossoms are done, they will turn a light pink, edged with a darker rose hue at the tips. Carefully remove each flower as it dries and gently set it aside.

    Ca Repeat the process for the long-stemmed roses. When these are done, they will be golden yellow with rosy coral edges.

    Ca To assemble this lovely token of friendship, tie a bow around the neck of the rose oil bottle with the three-quarter-inch-wide French wire ribbon. The beauty of French wire ribbon is in its flexibility. You can easily bend it into a saucy bow by shaping and spreading it with your fingers.

    Ca Line the gift box neatly with the rose-colored tissue paper, allowing generous flaps to overhang.

    Ca Fold the linen finger towel or table napkin so that it fits snugly in the box. If you have selected a towel with an embroidered or embossed edge, show the decoration face up. Lay the bottle of rose oil on the linen towel and scatter the tea roses around it, folding the tissue flaps gently over the arrangement. Place the note card on top and close the box.

    Ca The rose-sweet and rosemary-spice decorative arrangement

on top of a simple white box is one of my favorite ways to wrap a gift. Tie the one-and-one-half-inch-wide French wire ribbon around the box in traditional bundle style and form a knot. Center the sprig of fresh rosemary, then the four long-stemmed roses over the knot, and tie a generous bow. Allow the ribbon ends to swoop gracefully over the edges of the box.

One Dozen Perfect Rose Sachets

     ◌᷊ There is no such thing as too many rose sachets! I hang them in closets, place them in shoes and in the pockets of my suits and dresses, layer them in my lingerie drawer, scatter them in my armoire to scent my table linens, and when feeling truly inspired, I tuck them into ornamental pillows in my living room. I know you can dream up at least a dozen more uses for this versatile sachet.

6 fresh long-stemmed roses
12 cups rose potpourri
12 white lace-trimmed linen table napkins, luncheon size
8 yards pink faux-marble taffeta ribbon, 2/3 inch wide
Small spool white cotton kitchen string
1 sheet rose-print tissue paper
White long-stemmed rose box, available from a florist
2 yards green faux-marble taffeta ribbon, 2/3 inch wide

     ◌᷊ To hang-dry the long-stemmed roses, first remove the

thorns and most of the leaves from the stems, leaving one or two branches with leaves for contrast near the blossom. If you keep more than a branch or two on the stem, the drying time will take longer. Arrange the flowers into a bouquet, taking care to keep the stems separated, not entwined. Bind the bouquet together with a rubber band or string about an inch from the bottom of the stem end. Hook the top of a wire hanger through the rubber band or string so that the bouquet is suspended blooms-down. Hang the bouquet in a cool, dry place to dry for about a week. When the roses are dry, remove the rubber band or string and gently separate the roses. Set them aside to use for decorating the top of the gift box.

℘ Packaged rose potpourri comes in so many varieties, blends, and styles that it is virtually impossible for me to specify the amount you will need by a weight measure. Many mixtures combine berries, laurel leaves, and other herbs or spices, weighing more than a less complex blend of rose petals and lavender seeds. The wetness of the mixture is also a factor — the more oil, the heavier the blend. Instead, I have chosen to use a volume measure to determine the amount. You will need about one cup of potpourri per sachet, for a total of twelve cups to fill twelve sachets.

℘ For those of us who love to make every part of our gifts from scratch, I have a pure-and-simple potpourri recipe to try. From the better part of a one-pound bag of unscented dried rose petals, measure out twelve cups into a plastic bag. Add forty-eight drops of rose oil to the bag (four drops per cup of petals). Close the bag with a twist-tie or rubber band and toss gently for about a minute, mixing the petals to distribute the oil evenly. Set the bag aside in a cool dry place for several days. Once or twice a day, shake the bag gently to keep the oil evenly distributed. When you are ready to use the potpourri, remove it from the plastic bag, and place it in a large ceramic bowl.

❧ I like the formal, starched appearance that linen gives the sachets, so I use linen napkins. You may prefer a softer, more casual fabric. If so, cotton or chintz is a good choice. Avoid synthetics, as they can alter the fragrance of the potpourri. The size of the cloth you use should be larger than a tea- or dessert-size napkin, but not as large as a dinner-size, about ten inches square.

❧ Cut the pink ribbon into twelve equal lengths, each about two feet long. I like to use pinking shears to give the ends an interesting edge. Set the ribbon aside.

❧ Cut the kitchen string into twelve equal lengths, each about three inches long, and set them aside.

❧ Fold the tissue paper in half the short way. Tuck it into the long-stemmed rose box to line the bottom and the sides without overlapping the edges. Set the box aside.

❧ Clear a comfortable work area for yourself. Organize all your materials like this: the stack of pressed napkins open flat, the ribbon lengths, the string lengths, the bowl of potpourri, a glass

measuring cup, and the tissue-lined gift box. Place the first napkin in front of you. Scoop out one cup of potpourri and place it in the center of the napkin. Raise the corners and gather them together bundle style. Slide your hand down to pack the potpourri into a little pillow. Tightly tie the sachet closed with a piece of kitchen string, then let the corners of the napkin relax into a lacy fan. Wrap a length of pink ribbon around the string to cover, and bring the ends around to the front. Tie them securely, and make a pert bow.

☙ Place the first sachet inside the box, starting at a corner, not the middle of the box. Repeat this process until you have made all the sachets and filled the box. Don't try to force the sachets to fit side by side in the box. I have designed them to be placed diagonally in a pleasing zigzag pattern that fills the box snugly.

☙ Replace the top of the box. Wrap the green ribbon around the box to form a long cross, bringing the ends up to tie at the front. Lay the six dried long-stemmed roses on top of the ribbon crossing, and tie the ends around the roses securely. No need to finish with a bow — the half-dozen dried roses make a spectacular showing on their own!

Precious
Pressed-Rose Scented
Stationery

～～ Hearken back to the days before telephones, when friends and families shared warm thoughts, gossip, and other news with each other by writing letters. Precious Pressed-Rose Scented Stationery is the hallmark of genteel elegance — handmade paper, pressed floral whimsy, pride in a flowing hand, and a whisper of signature scent. The delicate fragrance of the tiny pressed rose blossom on each piece of unique scented stationery will inspire words unsaid — like snowflakes, no two roses are ever the same.

> *8 fresh miniature red roses*
> *Peach-colored, kid-finish, folded note-size stationery and*
>   *matching envelopes in a box with a clear plastic cover*
> *1 sheet rose-patterned wrapping paper*
> *Clear-drying white glue*
> *1 sheet white blotter paper, cut into 8 equal-size squares*

10 drops rose oil

1 yard maroon French wire ribbon, 1/2 inch wide

❧ Roses are especially difficult to press successfully because of the thickness of the rose hip. I have experimented with roses of every shape and size and discovered that miniature roses are the easiest to work with and never fail to press beautifully. Be sure to select roses that have matured to a nicely open bud on the way to full bloom. Trim back the stems to a three-inch length, retaining one or two branches of leaves for decoration.

❧ If you do not have a flower press, a heavy phone directory will work just as well. Open the book to the middle, slip a piece of blotter paper into the book, place the rose in the center of the blotter paper, and cover it with a second piece of blotter paper. You can also use tracing paper. (Don't use paper towels, because the puckered texture will be pressed into the surface of the flower as it dries.) Skip forward about ten pages in the book, and repeat the layering process for the remaining seven roses. Place another book on top of the directory for extra pressure, and set aside for about two to three weeks, until the roses are thoroughly dried.

❧ The folded note-sized stationery with envelopes comes in sets of twenty to the box, but the thickness of the pressed roses that you will be affixing to the front fold of the stationery will permit only eight pieces of stationery and eight envelopes to be placed in the box for your gift.

℘ Remove the stationery and the envelopes from the box and set them aside in a clean place.

℘ Cover the bottom and the sides of the stationery box with rose-theme wrapping paper. This is a lovely way to personalize your gift. The technique is similar to gift wrapping a package. Open the wrapping paper and lay it flat, with the pattern face down. Place the bottom of the empty stationery box in the center. Lift the sides of the wrapping paper up. Neatly trim the paper to a size that will cover the four sides of the box and leave one-half inch to fold over the inside edges. Brush the bottom and the long sides of the box with a thin, evenly distributed layer of glue. Be sure not to use too much glue when you paste the paper in place to avoid lumps forming under the surface. Paste the paper to the bottom and the long sides of the box first. Burnish the surface with a spatula or a dull butter knife to smooth away any wrinkles. Repeat this process to glue the short flaps in place, burnishing the surface to smooth. Cut little V-shaped darts at each corner to allow the remaining one-half inch of paper to fold easily over, accommodating the corners of the box.

℘ Cut the blotter paper to fit comfortably in the bottom of the box, approximately three inches square. Pinking shears will give the edges of this puffy paper a charming ruffled finish. Distribute the oil on the blotter paper, two drops on each corner and two drops in the center. Put the blotter paper in the bottom of the box and add eight envelopes and eight pieces of stationery. Replace the plastic cover. In the time it takes to press the roses, the scented blotter paper will have imbued the stationery with a marvelous aroma.

❧ When the roses are dry, remove the scented stationery and envelopes from the box. Arrange the pressed roses on the front of each piece of stationery in a way that is pleasing — centered or tipped jauntily — it's up to you. Any stray leaves or single petals that have come loose can be placed as if they were falling from the bloom. Touch a bit of glue to the back of the flowers and the leaves. Use a toothpick to place the glue neatly along the shaft of the stem. Gently press the flowers, the leaves, and the stem on the stationery to affix securely. Allow the decorated stationery to thoroughly dry overnight, outside the box.

❧ Place the Pressed-Rose Scented Stationery back in the box and replace the clear plastic top. Tie the ribbon diagonally across the corners of the box, florist style, and finish it with your bow perched prettily in the upper left-hand corner.

ROSY POSY
NAPKIN TIES

❧ Happily for lovers of the lavish, the romantic rococo style is back in vogue — frills, bows, fringes, bright pinks, and, in particular, a profusion of rose motifs blooming in every room. I can just imagine Madame de Pompadour using Rosy Posy Napkin Ties to highlight each place setting at one of her legendary dinner parties. The combined fresh scents of rosemary, cinnamon, and roses are a delightful way to stimulate everyone's appetite. If you can't help but keep the Rosy Posy Napkin Ties for yourself, then use them as part of your own rose-theme tabletop — a filled-to-bursting vase of full-blown roses as the centerpiece, sparkling goblets of Rosé wine, a rose damask tablecloth, and touches of dusty-rose china to form the backdrop for a gala rose fest.

Makes four napkin ties
12 fresh miniature blush-pink roses
16 inches green floral tape
4 yards leaf-green French wire ribbon, 1 inch wide
4 sprigs fresh rosemary, about 3 inches long

4 cinnamon sticks, about 4 inches long

4 cloth table napkins, dinner size

Matching tablecloth

2 sheets of leaf-green tissue paper

White gift box, dress size

3 yards deep-pink organdy ribbon, 2 inches wide

✺ Select the fresh roses carefully. Live roses are important here, even if you plan to dry the roses to give the napkin ties as a gift. Choose pink ones with matching hues and partially open buds. I like to use the Cecile Brunner rose with its tiny but perfectly formed flowers, but other miniature varieties will do nicely, too. You will need three miniature roses for each napkin tie.

✺ Remove all of the thorns and leaves from the stems, except one or two small leaves if they are growing near the bloom and not scarred. Cut the stems so that the roses measure about one inch from the top of the flower to the tip of the stem end. Set the roses aside.

✺ Cut the floral tape into eight two-inch pieces. You will need two two-inch pieces for each napkin tie. Set aside.

✺ Cut the French wire ribbon into four pieces, each one yard long, and set aside.

✺ To assemble the napkin ties, line up the four cinnamon sticks on a flat surface with their curled ends up. Position a sprig of rosemary along the center of the first cinnamon stick. Wrap a two-inch piece of floral tape around the middle of the sprig to hold it in place. Position three tiny rosebuds on top of the tape, binding the rosemary to the cinnamon. Secure the roses in place with a second piece of tape, bound as closely as possible to the section where the stem tip meets the rose hip. If you have left a leaf or two on the stem, lift them to lie flat behind the rose, to cushion the bloom like a pillow. If the leaves are left sticking out at the sides, they will crumble and become discolored as they dry, ruining the effect. If you have any doubts about the leaves, remove them entirely.

ᑎ᎒ Now, wrap the French wire ribbon once around the center of the cinnamon stick, rosemary, and roses to conceal the tape. Bring the ribbon ends back around to the front and tie a knot, then finish with a perky bow. Don't make the bow too large. You will need two long ribbon streamers, about seven inches each, to tie around the back of the table napkin, holding it in place. Repeat this procedure for each of the remaining napkin ties. Set the ties aside in a safe place to dry, about three to five days.

ᑎ᎒ Everyone has a favorite napkin fold, but for this presentation I suggest the following style: Fold the table napkin in half to form a square. Find the center point and grasp it. Lift and gently shake. The napkin will fall naturally into a soft, upside-down cone shape. Lay the cone on a flat surface, pointed end toward you. Place the napkin tie on the napkin, somewhere slightly below the center, toward the point of the cone. Tie the ribbon ends around the napkin, and knot them loosely at the back. For an elegant finish,

curl the ends of the French wire ribbon into springy waves on either side of the napkin. Repeat this procedure for each of the remaining napkins.

❧ Line the gift box with a double sheet of leaf-green tissue paper, allowing the long ends to overhang the sides. Fold the table-cloth flat to fit easily in the bottom of the gift box. Spread the napkins, decorated with the napkin ties, in a fan pattern on top of the tablecloth. Fold the tissue ends to cover the napkins and tablecloth. Replace the top of the box. Decorate the box by tying the deep pink organdy ribbon, bundle style, ending with a bow as big as Versailles.

❧ If you are planning to use the napkin ties to create your own rose-theme tabletop, choose the roses on the day of your party, assemble the spicy-rose ornaments, and tie them to the napkins right away. Place them in your refrigerator until just about one half hour before your guests are due. The rosebuds will open at the table and be in full bloom by meal's end.

MY LADY'S
BEAU CATCHER

প্ত A beau catcher, more common-
ly known as a rose jar, is a crock or ceramic container filled with a
moist or "wet" potpourri that will remain fragrant for years and
years. Dainty Victorian ladies employed its powers to entice their
gentlemen friends to act like rogues. Lift the lid and the intoxicating
aroma of blooming roses thrills the air. The scent never needs to be
enhanced with oils or the addition of fresh ingredients if you keep it
covered when not in use. I like to use blooms with some sentimental
value for potpourri prepared this way, since the scent will remain
alive for decades. It is an everlasting way to preserve a special bouquet of roses, perhaps from your valentine, or to share a part of the
prize-winning yield from a bush grown in your own garden with a
fellow rose aficionado.

10 large red garden rose blossoms, enough petals to fill a
   quart-size container
1/2 gallon-size stoneware crock with lid or ceramic ginger
   jar with top

Saucer, diameter to fit inside 1/2-gallon crock

1/2 cup sea salt

3/4 ounce ground cinnamon

1/2 ounce ground cloves

1/2 ounce ground allspice

1/8 ounce ground mace

1/8 ounce ground nutmeg

1/2 ounce orris root

2 ounces lavender flowers

1/2 ounce lemon verbena

20 drops rose oil

1 ounce rose water

Covered basket with super-tight weave, approximately
      6 inches diameter x 3 1/2 inches deep

5 dried red tea rose buds

2 yards blush-pink silk ribbon, 1/4 inch wide

1 yard light-green silk ribbon, 1/4 inch wide

   ॐ A "wet" potpourri is the equivalent of a floral marinade. The length of time that you allow the ingredients to blend and macerate undisturbed will determine the strength and longevity of the scent. A truly potent Beau Catcher will retain its fragrance for twenty years! Allow a month for the process to reach completion.

   ॐ Select fragrant roses in full bloom and wide open, with the petals ready to drop. Pluck the petals from the roses and lay

them in rows, spread out on paper towels to absorb any dew or moisture that may still cling to them. Be sure no beads of liquid remain on the petals, since excess moisture at this stage will cause the potpourri to develop mold. Ten roses should yield about one quart of petals, but if necessary, use another rose or two.

℘ Place a one-half-inch layer of petals at the bottom of the crock. Sprinkle with salt to cover. Repeat this layering and sprinkling process until you have used all the petals. Fit the saucer into the crock on top of the petals. Weigh it down with a stone or some other heavy object. Cover the crock and set it in a cool, dry place for ten days. Once a day, uncover the crock, lift the saucer out, and stir the mixture gently with a wooden spoon. Do not worry about disturbing the layers. Remember to replace the weighted saucer after each stirring. As time passes, the drawing action of the salt will cause some liquid to bubble to the surface of the mixture. Discard the liquid by pouring it off, not by forcing it out by squeezing or pressing down. The mixture will, and should, retain some moisture.

℘ On the tenth day, remove the salt-cured petals from the crock and set them aside. In a separate glass bowl, combine one-half ounce of cinnamon, the cloves, and the allspice. Cover the bottom of the crock with a layer of the mixed spices. Place a layer of the salt-cured petals on top and cover them with a layer of spices. Continue to sandwich the spices between layers of petals until you have returned them all to the container. Cover the crock and set it in a cool, dry place to finish maturing for three weeks.

◕✧ Your Beau Catcher is almost complete. In a separate glass or ceramic bowl, combine the remaining cinnamon, the mace, nutmeg, orris root, lavender flowers, and lemon verbena. Remove the spice-cured rose petals from the crock and add them into the mixture. The petals will be limp and moist. Add the rose oil, then add the rose water a bit at a time, starting with about one-half ounce. Use more if necessary, but remember that you want to moisten the mixture, not soak it. Toss and stir well with a wooden spoon to coat and combine all of the ingredients thoroughly.

◕✧ Transfer the potpourri to your woven gift basket. Pack it down tightly to about two-thirds full. Sprinkle the dried rosebuds on top to delight the eye every time the lid is lifted. Use any leftover potpourri for yourself by placing it in decorative covered containers around the house.

◕✧ Decorate the lid of the basket by creating a ribbon bouquet to sit cheerfully on top. Start by cutting eight inches off one end of the pink ribbon. Set it aside. Now take the green ribbon and the remaining pink ribbon and loop it around the width of four fingers of your left hand (right hand if you are left-handed). You will have more pink ribbon than green to loop around your fingers. Slide the ribbon loops off your fingers, and catch them in the center by tying with the piece of pink ribbon set aside. The result will be a floppy ribbon bouquet.

Finally, cut several of the loops open to form streamers that will dangle over the sides of the basket.

🙶 If you have chosen a basket with a handle on top of the lid, you can tie the ribbon bundle in place. If not, sew the bundle securely on the top of the basket lid with matching pink thread.

🙶 Traditionally, the Beau Catcher is housed in a covered ceramic container. You can do this, too, if you like, but I much prefer the homespun presentation of an artfully woven basket. As long as you don't leave the cover off the container for more than a half hour at a time, the potpourri will remain fragrant for years. Whichever presentation you choose, the results are the same — a heavenly aroma to fill the air with roses remembered.

LAST ROSE OF
SUMMER PERFUME

❧ Essential oil of rose is a star among fragrances. Its heady scent is the prized "heart-note" in the finest French perfumes. Imagine a fragrance that starts off tantalizingly floral, but tangy with a twist of spice, then becomes beguiling warm, as it releases the classic combination of musk and sandalwood, and you will have conjured up the harmonious blend of the Last Rose of Summer Perfume. I think of this romantic perfume as an heirloom scent, honoring the last blossoms on my favorite rosebush — the most precious ones of the year. The compelling scent of roses is truly inspiring, and the recipient of this lovely perfume will think of you truly and sweetly.

Makes one-quarter ounce

68 drops rose oil
8 drops sandalwood oil
6 drops bergamot oil
4 drops musk oil
Diluent to fill a 1/4-ounce bottle, approximately 34 drops

Glass eyedropper

1/4-ounce glass bottle with lid

1/4-ounce perfume flacon with atomizer top

Perfumer's funnel

᳭ The Last Rose of Summer Perfume is a blend using four basic scents. The tangy aroma of bergamot greets you first, but vanishes soon after the perfume is applied; velvety rose, the richest scent, gives the perfume its body and dominates the blend; and finally, the bewitching bouquet of sandalwood and musk, the most long-lasting scents, lingers delightfully on your skin all day.

᳭ Begin this project by arranging all of your essential oils and perfumer's tools around you like the great "noses" of Europe's world-famous fragrance houses do. Using the eyedropper, drop the rose oil into the quarter-ounce glass bottle. Clean the eyedropper with a small amount of diluent, then get it as close to dry as possible. Cleansing the dropper before adding each new oil to the mixture helps prevent tainting. Add the sandalwood oil, the bergamot oil, and the musk oil to the mixture, cleansing and drying the eyedropper between delivering each new oil to the blend.

᳭ The diluent is a form of unscented alcohol and glycerin that is used to stabilize and preserve the scent of a perfume. Carefully drop or pour in the diluent until you have filled the quarter-ounce bottle almost to the top. The blended perfume will appear to be nearly colorless, with a blush tint of yellow-gold.

ᘒ Seal the bottle and gently shake it to mix the ingredients together thoroughly.

ᘒ A beautiful perfume bottle will add spirit and style to its contents. Selecting the perfect bottle is fun, since there are so many shapes and varieties to choose from. Think about the qualities of the rose aroma you have mixed, then make your choice. For example, I find that the carefree mauve and white swirls of a hand-blown Venetian glass bottle capture the romantic mood of roses perfectly. A spray atomizer closure, with a push-button top or tasseled squeeze ball, is a marvelous way to apply rose-scented fragrance as a light mist.

ᘒ Once you have chosen your decorative atomizer, you are ready to decant the precious liquid into it. With the help of a perfumer's funnel, pour in the liquid by degrees. If you haven't worked with a perfumer's funnel before, be aware that it fills up quickly, but empties its contents slowly. Replace the atomizer top and set the flacon aside in a cool, dry place to age for at least forty-eight hours.

ᘒ The Last Rose of Summer Perfume will improve with age like a vintage wine. By the time you are ready to give this gift, all of the essential oils will have combined and bonded together to become a single, but delightfully complex, symphony of scent.

Rose Garden
Milk Bath Basket

∾ I love the look of appreciation that fills the eyes of my house guests when they see the luxurious surprise I've prepared for them. I transform the guest bathroom into a fragrant fantasy rose garden, complete with an indulgent Rose Garden Milk Bath to float away the weariness of travel. The aroma of rose oil soothes the body and the mind, and the rosewater after-splash is a cleansing finish to a relaxing soak. The dreamy scent of roses, rising from a steaming bath of milk-silkened water, will give your friends a rejuvenating experience and a fond memory of their stay in your home.

1 cup powdered milk
15 drops rose oil
Rose-patterned washcloth
12 inches red satin ribbon, 1/4 inch wide
Small cream-colored note card, 4 inches long x 2 1/2 inches
*   wide*
Chisel-point, felt tip pen with maroon ink

Medium-size straw basket
Small bunch baby's breath
Small bed floral moss
Rose-scented bar of soap
Rose water in a spray-bottle atomizer
Small bouquet of fresh garden roses in a round vase

ᑦᐧ Pour the powdered milk into a mixing bowl. Add the rose oil, stirring to combine completely. Spread the washcloth open on a flat surface, and spoon the mixture into the center. Gather the four corners of the washcloth together to form a bag. Tie it tightly closed with the ribbon, finishing with a sweet bow.

ᑦᐧ Write the following message on the note card:

"Enjoy a delightful Rose Garden Milk Bath. As you run your bath, drop this bath bag into the water. Squeeze it underwater to release fragrance and softness. If you wish, pull the petals from a fresh garden rose and float them on the water while you bathe. Afterward, mist yourself all over in a cloud of rose water.

Love, _____ "

ᑦᐧ I like to use a chisel-point, felt-tip pen to give my handwriting the polished look of calligraphy.

ᑦᐧ In the straw basket, use enough baby's breath and fresh green moss to line the bottom with a woodland cushion. Arrange the bath bag, the rose-scented soap, the rosewater atomizer, and the note card in the basket. Place the vase of roses nearby. Rose-pink towels

and a postcard reproduction of a floral painting mounted in a small silver frame will complete the bathroom's rose-garden tableau.

❧ When it's your turn to be the perfect house guest, for house warmings, or to calm the happy but invariably frazzled nerves of a new mother, you can transform the Rose Garden Milk Bath into a portable rose-theme luxury soak. Simply follow the bath basket assembly instructions, then place the basket in the center of a fluffy pink hand towel. Gather the four corners of the towel together, and secure them with a French wire-ribbon bow tied around a fresh and full-blown long-stemmed rose.

ROSE OF CASABLANCA
LOVE BEADS

❧ The fragile beauty of a rose bloom protected by a stem of "virtuous" thorns is a universal metaphor for innocent love and a romantic heart. The Rose of Casablanca Love Beads have a fascinating history. Some say the rose talismans were brought back from the Holy Land after the Crusades, others claim they were the first rosary beads. However, their mystical origins cannot be ignored. This marvelously fragrant chain of beads and precious charms can be worn as a necklace, carried in a pocket or purse for luck, fingered in times of stress like worry beads, or hung on the wall in a private corner of your room. The hypnotic scent of roses will rise from the beads as you fondle them to inspire the mind and warm the heart.

> *6 to 8 fresh large red garden rose blossoms, petals only*
> *Cast-iron skillet*
> *6 ounces rose water*
> *10 drops rose oil*
> *3 bamboo skewers*

2 1/3 yards red satin cord

5 charms or spiritual tokens

Small white gift box, 3 1/2 inches long x 3 1/2 inches wide
   x 2 1/2 inches deep

1 sheet red tissue paper

Rose-motif sticker

   The perfect time to begin to make this lovely rose jewelry is over a long weekend. The rose bead cooking and preparation time is about forty-eight hours, and the drying time, demanding some attention, about a week. Do not let this commitment deter you — the finished results are stunning.

   Carefully pluck the petals off the blossoms. Chop them very fine. The finer you chop, the smoother the texture of your rose beads. Place the chopped petals into the cast-iron skillet. Pour in the rose water. Add some tap water, if necessary, so that the liquid just covers the petals. Simmer over a low heat for one hour, never allowing the mixture to boil. Stir occasionally. When the mixture begins to turn black, turn off the heat. Let the mixture sit on top of the stove overnight. (I have suggested letting the mixture stand overnight because this routine fits nicely into my schedule. The optimum sitting time between simmers is six to eight hours.)

   The next day, repeat the process. This time, do not use rose water. Instead, add tap water to cover if necessary. Simmer for one hour. Turn off the heat and let the mixture stand again for six to eight

hours or overnight. As the mixture heats and absorbs the iron from the surface of the skillet, its color will turn from a rosy-red to a deep, rich purple hue, almost black. In effect you are creating blackened roses.

✍ Repeat the simmering process again on the third day. This time, add rose oil to the tap water to intensify the scent that may have evaporated from the heating and cooling. When the mixture is cool enough to handle, you are ready to begin forming the beads.

✍ On a flat surface, place a thick layer of paper towels to dry the rose beads on. Rub a little Vaseline or any moisture-barrier cream on your hands to prevent them from staining. Be sure to protect your hands from the unbelievably potent rose dye this cooking process produces. If you prefer, you can wear thin rubber gloves. Pluck a bit of the mixture from the batch and roll it in the palm of your hand to form a ball about the size of a large grape. Do not make the balls too small because they will shrink as they dry to about half their size when wet. Place the wet bead on the paper towel mat. Repeat this process until you have used all of the mixture. You will end up with sixteen to eighteen rose beads. Let the beads dry overnight. The paper mat will draw a lot of liquid from the beads as they dry.

✍ The next day, the beads will still be quite moist but firm enough to pierce gently with a wooden skewer. Place six beads about one-quarter inch apart on each skewer. Stand the skewers upright by wedging them securely into a basket, so the beads can dry in the circulating air. Set the basket aside, out of harm's way, for two or three days. Once a day, gently twist the beads on the skewer to prevent them from sticking and to make a nice-sized hole in each bead. When dry and ready to be removed from the skewers, each bead will have shrunk to the size of a large pea.

❧ Gently slide the beads off the skewers and set them aside. Cut a length of satin cord, about one and one half yards long. Pinch the end of the cord and thread it through the hole of the first bead. Slide the bead to the center of the cord and make a loose knot on either side to hold it securely, but not rigidly, in place. Tie your knots so that they are about half the size of the bead.

❧ Now think about the design you want to create with a pretty chain of beads, knots, and charms. Charms or tokens add a wonderfully personal touch to your chain of rose beads. You can choose I Ching coins, religious symbols, milagros, the Star of David, votives, crystals, dice, hearts, or whatever you think will add special meaning to this magical gift. Count the number of beads you have left after stringing the first one, and the number of charms you have decided to use, and lay them out in the pattern you like. I like the look of a charm placed after every third bead, but the creative decision is yours. String the beads and charms, making a knot between each. To give an evenly spaced look as you string the rose chain, attach your charms first to one side of the center bead and then to the other, so that the pattern "grows" evenly along the chain. If the charm has a loop or hole at the top large enough for the cord to fit through, it will be easy to slide it on the cord. If it doesn't have a hole or a loop that is large, take a piece of matching thread, insert it into the charm's hole, tie the ends around the cord, and sew into place. Repeat the threading and knotting process until you have strung all of the beads and charms. To finish, tie a knot toward the end of the cord to whatever length you desire.

❧ When you wrap this exquisite token of friendship, pure and simple is the theme. I recommend placing the delicate strand of rose beads in a small white gift box, cushioned on a pillow of red tissue. Close the cover of the box and decorate the outside with a Victorian rose-motif sticker. Another lovely way to gift wrap this precious piece of handmade jewelry is to use a small satin or velvet pouch with a drawstring closure.

ENCHANTED CLOSET
ROSEBUD POMANDER AND
SCENTED SATIN HANGER

❧ Gifts lovingly given are gifts lovingly received. This useful, yet luxurious, pair of closet enhancements will enchant even the most practical of people. The rose scent of the pomander will last and last, emitting a whisper of fragrance to fill the air and touch all that hangs in your closet with its classic perfume. The scented, padded hanger is an innovative marriage of "scents and sensibleness," a protective bonus for your prettiest, but easily creased clothing.

Rosebud Pomander

❧ I enjoy hanging several of these simple-to-make and long-lasting rosebud-studded pomanders in my bedroom closet, where they freshen the air with a warm, intimate fragrance of roses.

Dried and scented miniature rosebuds, about 60 depending on their size

Styrofoam ball, 2 inches in diameter
Small glue gun
3 inches green floral wire
12 inches pink French wire ribbon, 3/4 inch wide
20 inches pink French wire ribbon, 1 1/2 inches wide

❧ You can buy dried miniature rosebuds by the bagful, scented or unscented. (See "The Rose Lover's Source Guide.") They come in an assortment of rosy hues, from pale pink to mauve to dark red. Don't worry about matching the color, size, or shape of the rosebuds you select to cover the Styrofoam ball. Your finished pomander will be gaily multicolored and have a marvelous bursting-with-buds texture.

❧ If you prefer, use unscented dried rosebuds and scent them yourself. It is easy enough to accomplish. Place the required number of buds into a large plastic bag. Drop in ten to fifteen drops of rose oil, close the bag, and gently shake so that the oil covers the buds evenly. Set the bag aside for a day or two, until the scent has completely permeated the rosebuds.

❧ To cover the surface of the pomander evenly, pick a starting point and work your way around to make an "equator." You will find that the stems of the rosebuds will pierce the surface of the Styrofoam very easily. Pack the rosebuds side by side so that they fit tightly together. Secure each bud with a bead of glue from the glue gun. Cover the bottom half of the sphere first, then the top

half. Be sure to leave a one-bud space at the top of the ball to make room for a wire loop and decorative bow finish.

ꙮ Form the floral wire into a U-shape. Insert both ends into the one-bud space you left at the top of the ball. Do not press down all the way. Leave enough of an arch, about one-half inch, to hold the tied and knotted ribbons. Seal the wire arch at both ends with a squirt of glue.

ꙮ To make the loop the pomander will dangle from, first thread one end of the three-quarter-inch-wide ribbon through the wire arch. Then tie and knot both ends of the ribbon together, forming a loop about five inches long. Place the knot at the bottom, snugly fitting it into the wire arch. Glue in place.

ꙮ To conceal the wire arch, the hanging-loop's knot, and any glue that may be showing, thread one end of the one-and-one-half-inch ribbon through the remaining space in the wire arch. Wrap the ribbon around once to cover the back of the arch and knot, then bring the ends of the ribbon around to the front. Tie them together, but do not knot them. Now, take the ends of the ribbon and make a bow. Shape it to sit saucily on top of the pomander. Trim the ends of the bow at an angle with pinking shears.

Scented Satin Hanger

ꙮ The Scented Satin Hanger is the perfect partner for your Rosebud Pomander. I came up with the idea for this unique use of potpourri one day as I was making a pomander for a dear friend whose beautifully organized closet is a work of art!

1 padded white satin hanger with a ribbon closure
2 cups fine-blended rose potpourri
Needle and white thread
30 inches pink French wire ribbon, 3/4 inch wide
2 sheets pink tissue paper
Rose-patterned paper gift bag

ℭℯ Untie the ribbon around the neck of the hanger, paying close attention to the way it is wrapped and attached, so that you can replace it exactly later on. Discard the ribbon. Remove staples, if any, and discard.

ℭℯ Slip the satin sleeves off the hanger. Remove the cotton batting from the sleeves and discard it. Fill the sleeves with pot-pourri. I have specified "fine-blended" potpourri, meaning a mixture without seeds, dried fruit, or spices which will give a course, bumpy texture to the arms of your finished hanger. Be sure to pack the pot-pourri evenly into the sleeves, pushing it in, a little at a time, to avoid lumps. A chopstick can be very useful for doing this. When the sleeves are tightly packed, work the arm of the hanger back into one of the sleeves by wiggling it back and forth until it is inserted completely. Repeat the process for the second sleeve. Use the needle and thread to sew the open neck of the hanger closed.

❧ Tie the pink three-quarter-inch ribbon — the same color as the ribbon you used for the pomander — around the neck of the hanger to form a decorative bow. If you carefully duplicate the style of the way the original ribbon closure was tied, all of your handiwork will be cleverly concealed.

❧ Finally, slip the loop of the pomander around the arm or the neck of the hanger to swing freely. Loosely wrap the enchanting pair in pink tissue paper and place carefully inside the rose-patterned gift bag.

The Rose Lover's Source Guide

ANGELICA'S TRADITIONAL HERBS & FOODS
147 First Avenue
New York, NY 10003
(212) 529-4335
•Essential oils; potpourri; dried herbs

ANTIQUE ROSE EMPORIUM CATALOG
Rt. 5 Box 143f
Brenham, TX 77833
•Old-fashioned bare-root garden roses

APHRODISIA
282 Bleecker Street
New York, NY 10014
(212) 989-6440
•Essential oils; potpourri; dried herbs

AROMA VERA
2728 South Robertson Boulevard
Los Angeles, CA 90034
(213) 280-0407
•Essential oils; potpourri; dried herbs

BELL'OCCHIO
8 Brady Street
San Francisco, CA
(415) 864-4048
Ribbons; potpourri

THE BODY SHOP BY MAIL CATALOG
45 Horsehill Road
Cedar Knolls, NJ 07927
(800) 541-2535
Essential oils; potpourri; dried herbs

CALYX & COROLLA CATALOG
1550 Bryant Street
San Francisco, CA 94103
(800) 877-7836
Fresh cut flowers

CASWELL MASSEY CATALOG
Catalog Division
100 Enterprise Place
Dover, DE 19901
(800) 326-0500
Essential oils; potpourri; perfumer's supplies

CZECH & SPEAKE CATALOG
39C Jermyn Street
London SW1 6JH
England
(44) 71-439-0216
Essential oils; potpourri; perfumer's supplies

DISCOUNT CRAFTS SUPPLIES CATALOG
4320 31st Street North
St. Petersburg, FL 33714
(813) 527-4592
Basic arts & crafts supplies

DOROTHY BIDDLE SERVICE CATALOG
Route 6
Greeley, PA 18425
(717) 226-3239
Floral tape; florist supplies; Styrofoam balls

FLORAL EXPRESS CATALOG
564 Mission Street
San Francisco, CA 94105
(800) 234-2151
Fresh cut flowers

FLORIS SHOPS CATALOG
703 Madison Avenue
New York, NY 10022
(800) J-FLORIS
Essential oils; potpourri; perfumer's supplies

GARDENER'S EDEN CATALOG
P.O. Box 7307
San Francisco, CA 94120
Potpourri; bottles, jars, and containers

GEARY'S CATALOG
351 North Beverly Drive
Beverly Hills, CA 90210
(800) 243-2797
Potpourri; bottles, jars, and containers

GILBERTIE'S HERB GARDENS COMPANY CATALOG
Sylvan Lane
Westport, CT 06880
(203) 227-4175
Essential oils; potpourri; dried herbs

HEARTLAND CRAFT DISCOUNTERS CATALOG
941 South Congress Street
Geneseo, IL 61254
(309) 944-6411
Six thousand arts & crafts items; ribbons of every kind

HOVE PARFUMEUR LTD CATALOG
824 Royal Street
New Orleans, LA 70116
(504) 525-7827
Essential oils; potpourri

KIEHL'S PHARMACY
109 Third Avenue
New York, NY 10003
(212) 677-3171
Essential oils; perfumer's supplies

KRAFTMAN & ASSOCIATES CATALOG
Box 8042
Van Nuys, CA 91409
(213) 366-1090
Arts & crafts supplies; Styrofoam armatures, adhesives

POTTERY BARN CATALOG
P.O. Box 7044
San Francisco, CA 94120
(415) 421-3400
Potpourri; bottles, jars, and containers

ROSES OF YESTERYEAR AND TODAY CATALOG
802 Browns Valley Road
Watsonville, CA 95076
(408) 836-9051
•Old-fashioned bare-root garden roses

SAN FRANCISCO HERB COMPANY CATALOG
250 14 Street
San Francisco, CA 94103
(800) 227-4530
•Herbs; dried flowers; potpourri supplies

SMITH & HAWKEN CATALOG
25 Corte Madera
Mill Valley, CA 94941
(800) 776-3333
•Ribbons; potpourri; bottles, jars, and containers

TAIL OF THE YAK
2632 Ashby Avenue
Berkeley, CA 94705
(415) 841-9891
*•Ribbons; silk, wax-dipped, and papier-mâché roses;
peg alphabet sets*

VANGUARD CRAFTS, INC. CATALOG
1701 Utica Avenue
Brooklyn, NY 11234
(718) 337-5188
•Basic arts & crafts supplies

WELEDA INCORPORATED
841 Main Street
Spring Valley, NY 10977
(914) 356-4134
• *Essential oils*

ZIMMERMAN'S DISCOUNT CRAFT SUPPLIES CATALOG
2884 34th Street North
St. Petersburg, FL 33713
(813) 526-4880
•*Fifty-two-page catalog for every type of craft project*

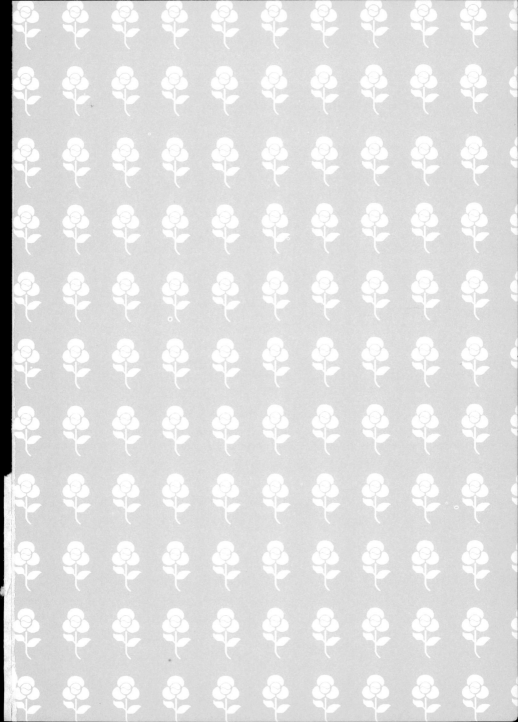

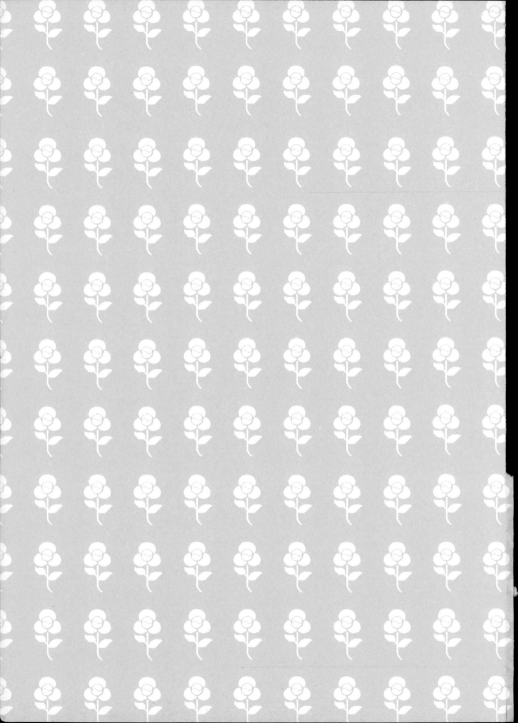